I0757691

Diary
2019

First edition 2019

Made by:
Literatura Angora.

Interior design and layout:
Literatura Angora.

Cover illustration:
Literatura Angora.

Images (CCO Creative Commons):
Pixabay.com

literatura-angora.blogspot.com

Diary
2019

Annual calendar

January 2019

	Su	Mo	Tu	We	Th	Fr	Sa
			1	2	3	4	5
	6	7	8	9	10	11	12
	13	14	15	16	17	18	19
	20	21	22	23	24	25	26
	27	28	29	30	31		

February 2019

	Su	Mo	Tu	We	Th	Fr	Sa
						1	2
	3	4	5	6	7	8	9
	10	11	12	13	14	15	16
	17	18	19	20	21	22	23
	24	25	26	27	28		

March 2019

	Su	Mo	Tu	We	Th	Fr	Sa
						1	2
	3	4	5	6	7	8	9
	10	11	12	13	14	15	16
	17	18	19	20	21	22	23
	24	25	26	27	28	29	30
	31						

April 2019

	Su	Mo	Tu	We	Th	Fr	Sa
		1	2	3	4	5	6
	7	8	9	10	11	12	13
	14	15	16	17	18	19	20
	21	22	23	24	25	26	27
	28	29	30				

May 2019

	Su	Mo	Tu	We	Th	Fr	Sa
				1	2	3	4
	5	6	7	8	9	10	11
	12	13	14	15	16	17	18
	19	20	21	22	23	24	25
	26	27	28	29	30	31	

June 2019	Su	Mo	Tu	We	Th	Fr	Sa
							1
	2	3	4	5	6	7	8
	9	10	11	12	13	14	15
	16	17	18	19	20	21	22
	23	24	25	26	27	28	29
	30						

July 2019	Su	Mo	Tu	We	Th	Fr	Sa
		1	2	3	4	5	6
	7	8	9	10	11	12	13
	14	15	16	17	18	19	20
	21	22	23	24	25	26	27
	28	29	30	31			

August 2019	Su	Mo	Tu	We	Th	Fr	Sa
					1	2	3
	4	5	6	7	8	9	10
	11	12	13	14	15	16	17
	18	19	20	21	22	23	24
	25	26	27	28	29	30	31

September 2019	Su	Mo	Tu	We	Th	Fr	Sa
	1	2	3	4	5	6	7
	8	9	10	11	12	13	14
	15	16	17	18	19	20	21
	22	23	24	25	26	27	28
	29	30					

October 2019	Su	Mo	Tu	We	Th	Fr	Sa
			1	2	3	4	5
	6	7	8	9	10	11	12
	13	14	15	16	17	18	19
	20	21	22	23	24	25	26
	27	28	29	30	31		

November 2019	Su	Mo	Tu	We	Th	Fr	Sa
						1	2
	3	4	5	6	7	8	9
	10	11	12	13	14	15	16
	17	18	19	20	21	22	23
	24	25	26	27	28	29	30

December 2019	Su	Mo	Tu	We	Th	Fr	Sa
	1	2	3	4	5	6	7
	8	9	10	11	12	13	14
	15	16	17	18	19	20	21
	22	23	24	25	26	27	28
	29	30	31				

January
2019

5 Jan
Saturday

6 Jan
Sunday

27 Jan
Sunday

28 Jan
Monday

February 2019

11 Feb
Monday

12 Feb
Tuesday

17 Feb
Sunday

18 Feb
Monday

March
2019

5 Mar
Tuesday

6 Mar
Wednesday

9 Mar
Saturday

10 Mar
Sunday

April
2019

11 Apr
Thursday

12 Apr
Friday

May
2019

11 May
Saturday

12 May
Sunday

15 May
Wednesday

16 May
Thursday

23 May
Thursday

24 May
Friday

June
2019

5 Jun
Wednesday

6 Jun
Thursday

25 Jun
Tuesday

26 Jun
Wednesday

July
2019

17 Jul
Wednesday

18 Jul
Thursday

August
2019

7 Aug
Wednesday

8 Aug
Thursday

September 2019

29 Sep
Sunday

30 Sep
Monday

October 2019

5 Oct
Saturday

6 Oct
Sunday

November 2019

3 Nov
Sunday

4 Nov
Monday

December
2019

Notes

Notes

Notes

Notes

Phone
Book

25 Jan
Friday

26 Jan
Saturday

February
2019

March
2019

7 Mar
Thursday

8 Mar
Friday

9 Mar
Saturday

10 Mar
Sunday

April
2019

19 Apr
Friday

20 Apr
Saturday

May 2019

23 May
Thursday

24 May
Friday

June
2019

17 Jun
Monday

18 Jun
Tuesday

July
2019

5 Jul
Friday

6 Jul
Saturday

17 Jul
Wednesday

18 Jul
Thursday

August
2019

September
2019

29 Sep
Sunday

30 Sep
Monday

October
2019

9 Oct
Wednesday

10 Oct
Thursday

November 2019

December 2019

1 Dec
Sunday

2 Dec
Monday

15 Dec
Sunday

16 Dec
Monday

19 Dec
Thursday

20 Dec
Friday

Notes

Notes

Notes

Notes

Notes

Phone Book

February
2019

March
2019

25 Mar
Monday

26 Mar
Tuesday

April 2019

9 Apr
Tuesday

10 Apr
Wednesday

11 Apr
Thursday

12 Apr
Friday

May
2019

11 May
Saturday

12 May
Sunday

June
2019

9 Jun
Sunday

10 Jun
Monday

July
2019

5 Jul
Friday

6 Jul
Saturday

August
2019

September 2019

5 Sep
Thursday

6 Sep
Friday

9 Sep
Monday

10 Sep
Tuesday

29 Sep
Sunday

30 Sep
Monday

October 2019

November
2019

19 Nov
Tuesday

20 Nov
Wednesday

23 Nov
Saturday

24 Nov
Sunday

December
2019

Notes

Notes

Notes

Notes

Notes

Phone Book

February 2019

March
2019

5 Mar
Tuesday

6 Mar
Wednesday

13 Mar
Wednesday

14 Mar
Thursday

April
2019

3 Apr
Wednesday

4 Apr
Thursday

11 Apr
Thursday

12 Apr
Friday

19 Apr
Friday

20 Apr
Saturday

May
2019

3 May
Friday

4 May
Saturday

11 May
Saturday

12 May
Sunday

June
2019

9 Jun
Sunday

10 Jun
Monday

21 Jun
Friday

22 Jun
Saturday

July
2019

17 Jul
Wednesday

18 Jul
Thursday

21 Jul
Sunday

22 Jul
Monday

25 Jul
Thursday

26 Jul
Friday

August
2019

3 Aug
Saturday

4 Aug
Sunday

19 Aug
Monday

20 Aug
Tuesday

September
2019

October 2019

9 Oct
Wednesday

10 Oct
Thursday

November
2019

13 Nov
Wednesday

14 Nov
Thursday

December
2019

1 Dec
Sunday

2 Dec
Monday

7 Dec
Saturday

8 Dec
Sunday

Notes

Notes

Notes

Notes

Notes

Phone Book

February
2019

March
2019

5 Mar
Tuesday

6 Mar
Wednesday

7 Mar
Thursday

8 Mar
Friday

25 Mar
Monday

26 Mar
Tuesday

April
2019

7 Apr
Sunday

8 Apr
Monday

27 Apr
Saturday

28 Apr
Sunday

May
2019

3 May
Friday

4 May
Saturday

11 May
Saturday

12 May
Sunday

23 May
Thursday

24 May
Friday

27 May
Monday

28 May
Tuesday

June
2019

July
2019

15 Jul
Monday

16 Jul
Tuesday

21 Jul
Sunday

22 Jul
Monday

August
2019

7 Aug
Wednesday

8 Aug
Thursday

September
2019

October
2019

November 2019

December
2019

Notes

Notes

Notes

Notes

Phone Book

25 Jan
Friday

26 Jan
Saturday

February 2019

March
2019

9 Mar
Saturday

10 Mar
Sunday

25 Mar
Monday

26 Mar
Tuesday

April
2019

3 Apr
Wednesday

4 Apr
Thursday

11 Apr
Thursday

12 Apr
Friday

May
2019

11 May
Saturday

12 May
Sunday

27 May
Monday

28 May
Tuesday

June 2019

29 Jun
Saturday

30 Jun
Sunday

July
2019

17 Jul
Wednesday

18 Jul
Thursday

August
2019

1 Aug
Thursday

2 Aug
Friday

7 Aug
Wednesday

8 Aug
Thursday

September
2019

13 Sep
Friday

14 Sep
Saturday

29 Sep
Sunday

30 Sep
Monday

October
2019

5 Oct
Saturday

6 Oct
Sunday

November
2019

December 2019

15 Dec
Sunday

16 Dec
Monday

Notes

Notes

Notes

Notes

Notes

Phone Book

February
2019

March
2019

9 Mar
Saturday

10 Mar
Sunday

13 Mar
Wednesday

14 Mar
Thursday

April
2019

May
2019

3 May
Friday

4 May
Saturday

11 May
Saturday

12 May
Sunday

June
2019

5 Jun
Wednesday

6 Jun
Thursday

17 Jun
Monday

18 Jun
Tuesday

July
2019

August
2019

7 Aug
Wednesday

8 Aug
Thursday

19 Aug
Monday

20 Aug
Tuesday

September 2019

1 Sep
Sunday

2 Sep
Monday

25 Sep
Wednesday

26 Sep
Thursday

October 2019

November
2019

3 Nov
Sunday

4 Nov
Monday

19 Nov
Tuesday

20 Nov
Wednesday

December 2019

27 Dec
Friday

28 Dec
Saturday

Notes

Notes

Notes

Notes

Notes

Phone Book

February 2019

23 Feb
Saturday

24 Feb
Sunday

March
2019

April
2019

3 Apr
Wednesday

4 Apr
Thursday

15 Apr
Monday

16 Apr
Tuesday

19 Apr
Friday

20 Apr
Saturday

May
2019

3 May
Friday

4 May
Saturday

11 May
Saturday

12 May
Sunday

June
2019

5 Jun
Wednesday

6 Jun
Thursday

15 Jun
Saturday

16 Jun
Sunday

July
2019

August
2019

September 2019

19 Sep
Thursday

20 Sep
Friday

25 Sep
Wednesday

26 Sep
Thursday

29 Sep
Sunday

30 Sep
Monday

October
2019

November
2019

23 Nov
Saturday

24 Nov
Sunday

December 2019

Notes

Notes

Notes

Notes

Notes

Phone Book

February 2019

March
2019

5 Mar
Tuesday

6 Mar
Wednesday

9 Mar
Saturday

10 Mar
Sunday

April
2019

May
2019

11 May
Saturday

12 May
Sunday

June
2019

17 Jun
Monday

18 Jun
Tuesday

July
2019

5 Jul
Friday

6 Jul
Saturday

August
2019

September
2019

29 Sep
Sunday

30 Sep
Monday

October
2019

9 Oct
Wednesday

10 Oct
Thursday

November
2019

December 2019

Notes

Notes

Notes

Notes

Notes

Phone Book

February
2019

March 2019

April
2019

3 Apr
Wednesday

4 Apr
Thursday

11 Apr
Thursday

12 Apr
Friday

15 Apr
Monday

16 Apr
Tuesday

May
2019

3 May
Friday

4 May
Saturday

June
2019

July
2019

27 Jul
Saturday

28 Jul
Sunday

August
2019

1 Aug
Thursday

2 Aug
Friday

31 Aug
Saturday

September
2019

5 Sep
Thursday

6 Sep
Friday

21 Sep
Saturday

22 Sep
Sunday

25 Sep
Wednesday

26 Sep
Thursday

October 2019

November
2019

December
2019

31 Dec
Tuesday

Notes

Notes

Notes

Notes

Notes

Phone Book

February 2019

March
2019

21 Mar
Thursday

22 Mar
Friday

25 Mar
Monday

26 Mar
Tuesday

April
2019

May
2019

11 May
Saturday

12 May
Sunday

17 May
Friday

18 May
Saturday

June
2019

25 Jun
Tuesday

26 Jun
Wednesday

July
2019

17 Jul
Wednesday

18 Jul
Thursday

August
2019

23 Aug
Friday

24 Aug
Saturday

September
2019

21 Sep
Saturday

22 Sep
Sunday

October 2019

1 Oct
Tuesday

2 Oct
Wednesday

November
2019

15 Nov
Friday

16 Nov
Saturday

23 Nov
Saturday

24 Nov
Sunday

December 2019

15 Dec
Sunday

16 Dec
Monday

19 Dec
Thursday

20 Dec
Friday

23 Dec
Monday

24 Dec
Tuesday

Notes

Notes

Notes

Notes

Notes

Phone Book

Contact	Phone number

Contact	Phone number

Contact	Phone number

Contact	Phone number

Emails

Contact	Email

Contact	Email

Contact	Email

Contact	Email